# A Secret to a Happy Life:

## Mind

## Your

## Own

## Business

*Your Happiness is Your Business, Mind it like it Matters.*

## BY E.J. SANTOS

**Anam Cara Enterprises, Virginia Beach, VA**

D1403259

First edition copyright © 2011 Elizabeth J. Santos

All rights reserved.

No part of this publication may be reproduced, stored in retrieval system, or transmitted in any form or by any means, electronic, mechanical, photocopying, recording, or otherwise, without the prior written permission of the publisher.

ISBN: 978-0-9962057-1-9


Published by Anam Cara Enterprises,
Virginia Beach, VA


Design and layout by Ankit PK.

# TABLE OF CONTENTS

# PREFACE

## INTRODUCTION

Who is this crazy woman and where is she taking me?

Okay, so yes I have been called crazy by more than one person in my life. I take some pride in that because my idol and self-appointed mentor, Dr. Leo Buscgalia said on many occasions, "I like being called crazy. It gives me wide latitude for behavior!" I could not agree more! He also said, "When people think you're crazy they are far more forgiving." I have also found that to be the case, well at least in my case.

Why am I writing this book? Because it's fun! Yes, I'm a geek; you'll find that out as you continue to read through the pages of this written body of work. *LOL*. As you can see already this is an "atypical" introduction in a book. I am hoping you find the information herein to also be presented in an "atypical" fashion as well, if not at least entertaining, inspiring and uplifting.

The purpose of the book is to uplift! That's it. I'm not here to tell you what you're doing is WRONG or that I have all your answers, or "my way is the best way" for you to get to where you're going. Seriously? How could I possibly tell you the "best" way for you to get to where you're going? I have no idea where you're going, how you want to get there, how long you want to take, who you'd like to go with (if anyone), and what you'd like to do along the way.

So again, I'm telling you right up front, I do not have all your answers. As you can see, I believe in truth in advertising. **\*LOL\***. So if you're looking for a quick fix, silver bullet, wooden stake, magic wand, guru or a guaranteed sure-fire solution to what ails you, you're looking in the wrong place.

What I am offering to share in this book are some tips and tricks I have used with GREAT success, and some with not so much success, along my trail. I intend to do that by sharing with you some of my own personal stories, perspectives, experiences and "ah-ha" moments that have allowed me to be able to live from a place of appreciation and enjoyment of life. I'll also sprinkle in a few anecdotes from various teachers, mentors, authors and guru's I've either met, read their books, heard of, or read about somewhere along the way. I'll do my very best to give credit where it is due. When I am unsure of the source I'll make that clear or simply offer it up to one of the most well-known sources in the world, anonymous. These techniques have made my life easier, more meaningful, fulfilling, and ABSOLUTELY MORE FUN!!!

What I am hoping you find through reading this book is at least one of the following:

Relief

Perspective

Humor

Hope

Faith

Happiness

Enjoyment

Peace

Love

Inspiration

Something to laugh about or at, even if it's me! I do it ALL THE TIME!!

And, if you don't find any of these things don't blame me.... Your happiness is your business, not mine. ;)

Sincerely,
EJ

# ACKNOWLEDGEMENTS

I'd like to acknowledge a number of people without whose help this book would still just be words in my head.

**Karen Weisiger** you are an unwavering and allowing friend. Your kindness and generosity are continual agents of transformation in my life.

**John Gabriel** for arguing these principles with me long enough to bring a fresh perspective to my thinking and lots of laughter as well! Your honesty, humility, confidence, integrity and candor are always a breath of fresh air. You are a rare man. I didn't say you were perfect, just rare... ☺

Thank you to my **students and clients** over the years. A special shout out to those people who passed through the **Success Skills for Business Academy** from 2009-2012 while I was the facilitator. You all were not just my students; you were also my teachers and collaborators on this book. Your questioning of these principles provided a continual conversation that asked me to translate them into practical terms. This allowed more clarity to flow and made translating the principles into current language and applications possible. Those three years facilitating the academy was a magical time. I am forever grateful to each of you who passed through those doors. You have all contributed to this book and my personal transformation.

**Dorrie Thompson,** thank you for giving me the opportunity to offer the Academy at your agency. You have become a priceless business partner and friend. Your wisdom and adventurous spirit are akin to my own, encouraging me to explore professional and personal pursuits I might have otherwise passed up.

**Jason Salcido** for being such a great inquisitor throughout the writing process, you asked questions that helped me to formulate my thoughts into meaningful applications of these principles.

**Cheryl and Drew Barnes,** your example of best friends being married with a blended family is a constant reminder for me to focus on being a relationship person.

**John David**, thank you for giving me a Kindle e-reader for Christmas in 2013. Although I was really irritated with you at the time, that gift brought me into the 21$^{st}$ Century. That then sparked within me the idea to get my first book published in e-reader format. I want to also thank you for unwittingly irritating me out of my comfort zone. I especially appreciate you arguing with me over the principles in this book often enough for me to gain confidence in the timelessness and universality of them. Our relationship provided me with endless opportunities to practice and apply these principles in real time.

**Michelle and Gregg Burton**, thank you for reading the manuscript and guiding me through the next steps in moving forward. Your professional guidance and personal enthusiasm for this project was reassuring and re-energizing for me.

**Judi Blaze**, thank you for your expert editing and proofreading of this manuscript, and for maintaining my voice throughout the editing process. My intuition was right on (again) when I hired you on Elance. I could have not chosen a better partner in the editing of this book. ☺

# CHAPTER I
## Make Your Happiness Your Business

*"The Constitution only guarantees American people the
right to pursue happiness.
You have to catch it yourself."*
*- Benjamin Franklin*

## Taking Ownership of Your Happiness

I remember hearing this a lot growing up, "Take care of others and they'll take care of you." That translated to "Make others happy and they'll make you happy." So I take this advice and become a *people pleaser*. You know it starts VERY early. People want you to behave a certain way so they'll be happy and of course since I was a VERY well-trained and obedient girl, I'd do whatever was humanly possible to attempt this feat. Of course, also being human, I didn't hit the mark all the time and was reprimanded in one shape or form for *my short comings* in not being able to make someone else happy. I again was a good little soldier so I marched on, trying even harder the next time to get it right.

As long as I did not ask for anything, took what I was offered, and sacrificed my needs, wants and desires, everyone else was happy!! As a child this was easy to do because really, what else do kids have to do other than spend all their time making everyone around them happy, either by saying their name first, using the toilet, eating the god awful baby food they spoon into your mouth and act like you like it, or by playing chore child to everyone older.

Now I don't want you to think I had an awful childhood, I didn't, at least not in my mind. I grew up in the country and found nature and animals to be a great source of comfort and joy. I had daily opportunities to connect with them and did so often. But, you get my drift about making others happy. It took me a while to figure out that in those instances when I played the *pleaser* I was putting everyone else's happiness before mine. As an adult, the task of making others happy became far more daunting, and in most cases my track record for pleasing others was not all that great. Here is a rough estimate on the stats as an adult:

- About 50% of the time people were pleased and they *acted* like they were happy with me.
- 25% of the time no matter what I did, I could not make the other people happy.
- 25% of the time people were polite but I could tell they were not "happy" and frankly neither was I.

As an adult, I finally began to ponder and analyze this *edict* which soon begged the question, "Why is it I was not having stellar success with this *profound* wisdom of the ages?" The way I saw it, no one was happy for any length of time, at least not those I observed practicing this *tradition* anyway. I wondered if I was the crazy one or if they were? If it's not working why was I doing it? Let's explore this idea a little further.

E. J. SANTOS

# It's your job to make you happy, no one else's.

Okay, now some of you may be offended by this and others will be down-right furious because I'm letting this cat out of the bag. Those of you who are angry or bothered by this statement are likely narcissists, so we'll take your complaints with a grain of salt. ;) Allow me to explain what I mean by this statement.

This started to make sense for me while I was building a presentation on self-empowerment for a woman's conference where I was one of the presenters. One of my speaking points was letting go of old habits that no longer worked. I decided to use the popular definition of insanity—'Doing the same thing over and over again, expecting a different result.' All of the stars must have been aligned in that moment because the clouds parted and I saw the light. The light shined on my own habitual thinking and behaviors that kept me perpetuating this *tradition*. I saw the insanity in my thinking and habits!!! That was an AH-HA moment if ever there was one. Talk about self-revelation.

So, I had been keeping a belief alive around the phrase "giving is better than receiving" without understanding the full meaning of the phrase. I was raised to believe this meant giving to others, period. Isn't that what you were raised to believe or am I the only nut case? What I have discovered, through personal examination and observation of others, is that something was omitted in the translation.

They left out the part where giving included giving to myself as well. My happiness is just as important as everyone else's – this phrase will be repeated numerous times throughout this body of writing, so don't think it's a misprint. ☺

The other thing that has been neglected to be explained is; giving is better than receiving *when* you are of the mind of generosity. When giving *feels good* and is done without expectation of reciprocation, or a sense of obligation, and does not leave you deprived in your own well-being, <u>*then*</u> giving is better than receiving. By the way, the phrase "Give til it hurts" from my new perspective is ignorant (and was likely made famous by a narcissist).

***Your happiness must be of the utmost importance to You.*** Here is the reason why, because everyone else is too busy tending to their own business aka "happiness" to tend to yours. Now as I mentioned earlier, your happiness is just as important as everyone else's. Here is the catch, it will never be as important to anyone else as their own. They may have the desire to make you happy and probably do on many occasions. However if you are not already happy, little to nothing they do will *make* you happy. *This works both ways.* If another person is not happy, little to nothing YOU do will *make* him or her happy. We can only give what we have in abundance and happiness is certainly no different than any other commodity.

Okay so what does that mean? Well, some of you are not going to like this at all, but I'm going to say it anyway…. 'We are all narcissists'. Don't go ballistic on me, hear me out. This narcissism shows up in a variety of ways AND is not a bad thing. In fact, it is natural and normal. It can be expressed in unhealthy ways like when we (or they) expect everyone else to cater to us (or them) and we ignore our own happiness in lieu of theirs more times than not. That is over the top and unhealthy narcissism. A little goes a long way. ;)

When we expect others to relinquish their happiness, and manage ours (or we are the ones relinquishing ours to manage someone else's) several things tend to occur:

1. Happiness managers are expected to relinquish their own happiness in order to manage the seekers' happiness. When they don't, happiness managers are considered selfish. - Imagine that! ;)
2. Happiness seekers are satisfied for only short periods of time. Since these people really have no idea what makes them happy their demands are insatiable.
3. Happiness managers cannot seem to get it right, which is brought to their attention often by the happiness seekers. This is a by-product of #2.
4. Happiness seekers are not happy – This is a by-product of #2
5. Happiness managers are not happy – This is a by-product of #1

A rather vicious circle if you ask me and one I prefer to avoid. How about you?

Now, some people find happiness in these situations and perhaps that is you. If that is the case, I for one would never encourage you to stop doing something that truly makes you happy. Some people love co-dependent relationships and they are very functional and happy and all parties involved benefit from it. If that is you, don't stop!! You've got a good thing going, keep it going. Be happy! I am not kidding here. However, for those of you who are not happy in this type of relationship, keep reading.

Change can be uncomfortable and sometimes scary. I've been through all of this and risen like a Phoenix from the ashes more beautiful and authentic than ever before, every time. One thing I can promise is for as long as you are reading this book, I'll be with you every step of the way. You are not alone… ;)

## Saying YES to you!

Have you ever found yourself at an event or party, or in a situation asking yourself, "What the heck am I doing here?" or "How did I get here?" I'm not talking about having a little too much to drink and not remembering how you got home, although that certainly is valid. I'm talking about those times when you realized you're doing something, or you are with someone, and realize this was never your intended destination for your evening or your life. The next question is usually, "What was I thinking?"

In some instances these questions come up only minutes later and in others it is decades. Never fear, no matter where you are you can always make a new choice. The next thing to ponder is, "What advice or what belief got me here? What is driving this thinking?" When I find myself in these situations I realize that I was saying no to me and yes to someone else. I was going along with something to make someone else happy, or make their life better, thinking that would make me happy too. In some cases it did, just not the majority of the time, and I prefer to have the odds in my favor. Yes, there's that narcissism I mentioned….. ;)

Over time I have learned to listen to my own inner compass and have become more confident in my independent decision-making skills. There are times when I still doubt them and find it a little slow going and realize I've done it again. I've said yes to something I did not want to do and it involved another person's persuasion. If I just didn't have to deal with other people, my decisions would be much easier. ;) Then there would be no disappointing anyone, dealing with hurt feelings or bruised egos—you know how that goes. But then again, for me life isn't all that much fun doing things alone all the time. I like interacting, working and playing with others –so there's the catch, how to find a healthy balance. In those instances when I agreed to something I was not crazy about, I now realize that was a way of avoiding disappointing someone else. That is not to say there are never times when I choose to go along with someone else's suggestion that is not all that appealing to me. I do, and for any number of reasons. One is I want to be with that person. What we do together isn't as important as being able to spend time together, enjoying his or her company. Another reason may be it is something I'd never done before and sounds interesting. As long as the activity isn't degrading to me or others, illegal or against my personal morals, I give it a go. On a number of occasions I have been introduced to something new and came to like it, by saying yes to someone else. So remember, this is a principle not a rule and is fluid in application.

The point here is to pay attention to how you feel after you have agreed to something, especially if it goes against your first instinct or gut response to say no to it. When you do say yes to something and later realize it was a mistake, you can always get out of it. It's called *changing your mind* and goes along with MYOB. If you are afraid of hurting someone's feelings or offending them try this: You can call or go to them and say with sincerity "I know I agreed to do _____ with/or for you, however I have come to realize I am not going to be available /or I've over committed. I am sorry if you are disappointed, I just have some things I need to take care of which conflict with going to this event/or doing this thing with you or for you." Here is where integrity applies. You don't have to lie to this person and neither does it have to become a confessional!

At the first sign of feeling bad about agreeing to something, address it. I suggest you **not** wait until the last minute to tell the other person you're not going. That is likely to happen in the beginning, when you are first learning how to use this technique. However, do not make it a habit. If that *is your habit* - waiting until the last minute and ditching people - you are being disrespectful to both yourself and them. Now I don't want you beating yourself up over this either. Does this bad habit make you a bad person? I say, no. Are you doing this intentionally to hurt someone? I say, highly unlikely. It has been my experience and observations in these situations, that people are not thinking 'I'm going to say yes to this person just to dump them later to hurt them.' I have heard of some people doing it in retaliation from time to time after it's been done to them. However, I have never met a person who is mean-spirited by nature. They've either been programmed that way – taught to hate - or are the walking emotionally wounded. Everyone I have ever met (including me) has been disrespectful, it happens all the time. What I have come to understand about this phenomenon is, on the whole, it is unintentional. I've also realized, in many cases it is a by-product of what I call BPS; the Be Polite Syndrome.

We are trained at a very early age to "be polite." This is in general is a VERY good thing. I love well-mannered people and strive to be one myself. I am not telling you to stop being polite, and I am not knocking manners. What I am saying is, be mindful of what you are agreeing to and when you may be falling into BPS. BPS drives us to say yes to things for the wrong reasons. This includes and is not limited to; avoiding disappointing others, peer pressure/fear of rejection/wanting to fit in/seeking approval, avoiding other unpleasant things we've said "yes" to—and the mother of the all of them—because you feel guilty or obligated.

Okay, so if you're light bulb has not yet turned on, you're probably thinking what does this have to do with my own happiness? I say *everything*. Look, I am not advocating not caring about other people; that is not what I am saying at all. What I *am* saying is **your happiness is just as important as everyone else's**. **It is not anyone else's job to keep you happy AND, it is not your job to keep anyone else happy.**

## Self-Empowerment - Giving yourself permission to want and have what YOU want!

How many of you have heard the phrase 'ask and you shall receive'? I imagine some of you can even quote it from the book that made that phrase famous. However, do you really know how it works? Let's explore this a little.

I'm going to use ordering a coffee at a custom coffee house as an example. You walk in and think *I just want a cup of coffee*. While you wait in line you hear people placing these very complex coffee orders; "I'll have a tall, decaf, half soy half non-fat, sugar shot, with whip - coffee." In that moment, if you are thinking, '*How ridiculous is this person and who is he or she to be so demanding?*' I have been the person complaining myself and I've got news for you. If you are not getting what you want out of life, guess what, you're not asking for what you want when placing your order. If you have been settling because you have been trained to think this is as good as it gets, *yet feel as if there is more*, you are on to something. You see, the other half of that phrase I mentioned *'ask and you shall receive'* is *"if you don't ask you don't get."*

According to the Funk and Wagnall's dictionary, the definition of empowerment is "to authorize; delegate authority, and to permit." In short; *to give permission*. To some degree we have all been trained to think like many others before us. Again, my theory revolves around socialization, fitting in and being accepted. As children we are trained to think and act in ways that please others and help us "fit in." After all, if we didn't there could have been dire circumstances such as no food, no shelter, and other seemingly serious consequences like adult disproval, or shunning from neighborhood kids. We are trained from a very early age to appease others. Depending on how strong that influence was, or perhaps still is, as adults we continue that trained behavior and thinking. It can work very well for us in a number of situations, however when practiced out of habit rather consciously, it can cost us dearly in the long run. My perspective on this is tied to the idea that "it is better to give than receive." And as I mentioned before, it is wonderful to give to others and say yes to them, just remember to give to yourself and say YES to you too! Don't leave yourself out of your giving circle. ☺

## Putting your happiness First!

Have you ever been in a situation where you have a number of offers to do something with various people yet really all you want to do is stay home and relax by yourself? You may feel pressure from some of these people to choose *them* and their plans. This of course will make *them* happy, but how does it feel to you? Does it feel almost suffocating to be around these people at that time? If you've been raised to "be polite" and not let anyone down, you may now feel guilty or obligated to make them happy. When you do, do you usually have a rather crummy time and then wonder why in the heck you went? Do you perhaps beat yourself up for agreeing to the whole thing to begin with? If any of this sounds familiar to you, don't worry you're not alone AND there is an antidote. Here's a little secret I'll share with you. It feels terrible in these moments because your happiness was ignored or put at the bottom of your list of priorities.

I can hear it now… "Are you crazy?" (I'll leave that for you to decide). This kind of thinking goes against what most of society trains us to believe.

The basic societal training I picked up told me that what others think of me (and making them happy) is far more important than what I think of myself (and my own happiness). Does that sound familiar to anyone? I have come to realize that is one of the greatest falsehoods ever perpetuated. One of the ways I've recognized this as a falsehood is through dating. Yes dating. If you haven't noticed (and it may be difficult to discern just reading a book) I am a rather enthusiastic person. I love to laugh and I happen to have a very hardy and contagious laugh. Here's where it all began. When I was young (6-7 years old) I did not hold back my volume until one day my mother or her mother said to me, "Boys don't like loud girls." That statement was not meant to be empowering, it was meant to "help" me be more attractive to boys and get me to "quiet down." Can you believe it!? I know they meant well but….. sheesh, I was a kid…. and it's not Edwardian England or the 1800's. I don't need to be pleasing the male population at that age. Anyway, since I was a *people pleaser* and liked to see people happy, that tactic did get my attention. So for some time after, I was self-conscious about being loud.

My enthusiasm was hard to contain and I found myself struggling to do so. Since an adult told me this and they were the *experts*, I thought I'd better do it if I wanted to be *liked*. After a while I just dulled my enthusiasm a bit but it would still come out, and I was left with that awful feeling of *You did it again. You drove him away because you're so loud.* This became even more pervasive as time passed. I could not contain my enthusiasm to please others so I tried to do other things to accommodate men to make up for being loud. When I went on dates I would agree to things thinking it would make the man happy. After a number of dates we both realized neither of us was really happy and got bored with each other. When I started to take ownership of my happiness and put it first, things started to improve. What I have finally realized is, when I negotiate the date around my comfort and pleasure, the man tends to be more engaged and in most cases more relaxed and happier. This I have come to find out makes it easier for him too, because he doesn't have to try to read my mind! When I know what I like and can articulate that clearly (putting my happiness first), he tends to relax into the decision-making and negotiation process. We both have the opportunity to express what will make us happy in the moment and synergize rather than compromise. I'll save that for another book ;) In the end, we are both happier with the decisions when we are clear about what makes us happy and why we are together—to have fun!

Putting your happiness first does not mean ignoring everyone else's happiness. It means making sure your happiness is included and regarded with the same value and importance as everyone else's *equally*. No more, No less. ☺

# Chapter II
## Make Yourself Your Best Advisor

*"Believe nothing, no matter where you read it or who
has said it, not even if I have said it, unless it agrees
with your own reason and your own common sense."*
*- Buddha*

### Trusting yourself and your intuition

Have you ever had a hunch about something that came true? You
think of a person from your past, an old friend or a family
member then you receive a letter or a phone call from them or
about them? You heard your inner voice telling you to take a
different route driving home and you did, avoiding a major
traffic jam or accident? Or is it the other way around for you?
You heard the voice, ignored it and got stuck in that traffic jam
or accident? Are you able to hear that voice or feel those
feelings at all? Do you know how your intuition communicates
with you? Does it communicate as that "little voice" in your
head, or that "feeling" in your gut, or that Deja` vu vision or
dream, or an absolute "knowing"?

I cannot tell you how many times my intuition has been my
absolute saving grace and on the flip side, how many times I
have ignored it to my own peril. The problem first lay in my not
trusting my intuition, the second problem was not understanding
how my intuition communicates with me. I've come to realize
these two things are inextricably linked. Here's one thing you

can count on, your intuition is always in the ON position and I mean ALWAYS. I am not talking about instinct, such as *automatic responses* controlled by the brain in *fight or flight* situations, or *trained* motor responses. I am talking about mindful, conscious awareness and guidance. *There is a big difference.* If you have not yet consciously experienced that difference, you're missing out on one of the greatest tools you have at your disposal for minding your own business, finding your bliss, and living a happy life. I suggest that discovering how to get in touch with your intuition is your next assignment and learning journey. I'll share a few stories about how I've come to know, trust, and follow my own intuition.

## Listening to your inner voice – No you're not CRAZY!!

I can't recall where it all began because once I started to consciously pay attention to my intuition, I realized it had been communicating with and guiding me from a VERY early age. What I can recall are the times when I knew my intuition was coming through with no interference. Speaking of interference, I've also come to realize there is nothing that gets in the way of me and my intuition, other than me. There is no devil inside or outside of me telling me to do something that is harmful to me or others, it's all me. The big light bulb went on for me when I understood it's actually my thinking that causes the interference. This brings us back to the principle of *we get what we think about, believe and practice.* This happens whether we are conscious of it or not…. but now I digress. ;)

Okay, back to my examples of intuition in action. When I lived in Southern California I worked part-time in a book shop specializing in esoteric studies. As a staff member I was surrounded by people who practiced and taught esoteric arts professionally. I had many opportunities to attend these classes and so I did.

In one of the classes we were working with something called "programming" and that related to deliberately creating things, or making things happen. This is a technique used to guide you toward a desired result. It is not designed to manipulate people to your own ends. I've tried it and it doesn't work. Go ahead, if you want to see what happens just be ready to do some damage control later on down the line. I've given you fair warning. ;)

In the class we were given our weekly homework and the instructor suggested choosing something small and easy to practice with first. A friend of mine once mentioned getting really good parking spots by using this method, and since finding parking was something I grappled with daily, I decided to try "programming" parking. Here's the scenario:

I worked at the Mira Mar Sheraton in Santa Monica. This hotel borders residential areas on the north side of the complex, downtown Santa Monica on the south side, the Pacific Ocean cliffs on the west side, and another hotel on the east side. Parking was at a premium, with 2 hour metered parking on 3 sides, residential on the 4$^{th}$ and $20/day valet in the parking lot. I was not making a lot of money so the valet was out. The meters were difficult to manage because if the hotel was busy you couldn't just leave to "feed your meter," AND you have to set reminders to run out every two hours. The residential was tricky because of the time of day I worked. I had an early morning shift and most of the residents were still home when I came to work, making it even more challenging. So there is the scenario, what a perfect way to test this technique.

So here is how it went. I had a 15-20 minute drive to work, which I discovered was the perfect amount of time for me to make this work. Right before leaving my apartment I visualized the hotel and surrounding parking areas where I preferred to park. I would say, "Help me find *free parking* within 1 block of the hotel." I let that thought radiate out, continuing to visualize the area. I then started driving. Along the way I found myself hitting every green light (or in some cases, every red light) and when I arrived at the hotel I made one pass around the block and found a parking spot in my range. I did this every day for 3 years and found a spot in my range 95% of the time. The other 5% was when I forgot to program it, or was not clear in the programming. In those situations I found a metered spot and would move my car on my lunch break to a free spot 90% of that time.

Over time, what was really powerful for me in this exercise was not getting the parking space but learning how my intuition speaks to me. There were times when on my way to work I would find myself hitting every red light. I would start to get nervous about being late for work and not finding a good parking spot. Then I found myself thinking (hearing the voice in my head) *you have to give them time to clear your parking space. These delays are allowing for the perfect spot to be open when you arrive and you'll be on time.* I would then relax into the process and go with the flow. I found when I got to the area I would listen again for the guidance which led me to the right street, finding my parking in minutes.

After years of playing with this I find it much easier to hear and feel my intuitive communications and finding bigger and better circumstances, as well as events that lead to having a happy life. I now know and trust the difference between my intuitive guidance and my old habits of thinking. The old *programs*, which are not intuitive at all but are, in many cases, things I have been taught to think by others.

These are what I call *social programming*. They are beliefs, traditions and behaviors passed down to me by others in an attempt to help me "fit in" or behave in ways that make others feel better. This relates to what I mentioned earlier in the *putting your happiness first* section. The antithesis of trusting your intuition is behaving in ways just to please, or make others happy, especially when it feels awful.

Okay, so we all have intuitive inclinations and capacities, it is innate to all of us. I have not met a person yet who has not had an intuitive experience of some sort, even if they didn't use that label. What I have also seen is many of us being *trained* to believe that those of us having these experiences are *bad, evil, possessed or crazy;* Crazy being the biggest. If you hear voices in your head, you're crazy. Well, I was hearing a voice, so to avoid being *labeled* I learned to stop telling people about my experiences. The funny thing was I did not stop hearing my intuitive voice. I just put a damper on it and didn't trust it for a long time. The cool thing is though, it never went away. For that I am most grateful, relieved and happy, and can say I hear it loud and clear these days. And although some may call me crazy, as I have mentioned numerous times, I no longer find that a damning label, I find it liberating. For that liberation I again thank Leo Buscaglia, who passed away in 2002, for his words of wisdom in his audio tracks from Living Loving Learning; "I love being called crazy. It gives me a wide latitude for behavior." ;)

## Think for yourself, talk to your self

The think for yourself, talk to yourself principle does not apply to everyone. It is geared toward those of us who tend to "think out loud." ☺ For those of us who do (I include myself as I am a HUGE proponent of thinking out loud) this may save you a lot of explaining and reduce arguments and confusion in your closest relationships. It also reduces interference from others in your thinking processes. I'm not talking about avoiding conversation, but rather allowing your thoughts to freely flow without over analysis, dissection, or judgment (from yourself or others). Thinking out loud provides an opportunity to practice a conversation, dream in real time, and ask the hard questions without persecution or interruption. It also allows you to listen to yourself, which for me has been very eye opening, enlightening, humbling and empowering. I realize some of you may be thinking "she's crazy... talking to herself." I say thank you, since you know how I feel about being called crazy ;)

For those of you who are not as comfortable with the idea of being considered crazy, hopefully this will ease some of your discomfort. There is psychological research that suggests talking to yourself can be a very healthy practice. It is recommended by some psychotherapists as a way to think through tough issues and make better decisions. Because *you know you better than anyone else* on the planet, *you know what's best for you.* If that is not the case, I suggest you get to know you and what you want very soon. If you don't, you may find yourself living someone else's life and most likely feeling miserable and unhappy most of the time.

Here is what I've come to discover about listening to others, especially when I have not asked for their advice. When others disagree with my decisions and say "I would never dream of doing THAT" or "If I were you"… who do you think they are talking about? I have figured out they are speaking the truth and it is THEMSELVES they are talking about! *They* would *never* do what I'm doing, which makes it *wrong* for them.

However, that *does not make it wrong for me*. They are not me. Their dreams and their fears are theirs, not mine. I have also come to realize when someone else tries to tell me how to live my life, who to date, what job to take, what food to eat, etc., it feels "off" or uncomfortable to me because I know best what is best for me, not them. In those moments of discomfort or mental dilemma, I am discounting and disregarding my own guidance system, my intuition and intelligence. That is the reason why it feels bad to listen to others. Not because they are bad people giving bad advice, but because their advice just does not fit me in that moment. *It may work for them or someone else perfectly - it just doesn't work for me*

In many cases, many of us have been *programmed* away from listening to ourselves. This leads us to believe we are not our best decision makers, and that the *experts* know best, so we go along with their suggestions or recommendations. This is not a bad thing when applied deliberately and when the expert is someone we trust or respect. I am not telling you to ignore everyone else on the planet's advice, well maybe I am, but not in the way most would think. What I am suggesting is to go ahead and listen to others and then make your decisions based on what feels best to you *in relation to your intentions and desired results*. Go with what makes *you* happy and gives *you* relief. There were (and still are on occasion) times when I asked others for advice and realized I wasn't asking for advice but rather *looking for approval or agreement*. I wanted someone to give me permission to pursue my ideas. I did not trust myself and was afraid to fail. Again, I discounted my own ability to make good decisions about my own happiness. I'd been trained so far away from listening to myself I found myself *suffering from what I call "perfectionist paralysis."*

My definition of *perfectionist paralysis* is wanting absolute assurance of every success before making a decision, and taking any action on it. I wanted to know how the dance would end before I got on the dance floor. Sound familiar to you? I wanted to remove all of the ambiguity and uncertainty before deciding to take on a project. I am glad to say I have transcended my own perfectionist paralysis in those areas of my life where it was holding me back. That does not mean I take on projects and agree to everything without consideration. Not at all, it simply means I am now more confident in my decisions and better able to handle the ambiguity and uncertainty of situations. Because I trust myself to be able to take life as it comes, I am more willing to take on more of what life has to offer and take it in stride. I am also better equipped to step away from things that are not supportive of my goals and lifestyle. There is very little I have to prove these days so the chip is off my shoulder and the trust is in me.☺

Am I perfect? NO. Do I get it right all the time? NO. Do I get insecure about things? YES. I am no different from anyone else in those areas. The difference is in my ability to trust myself and give myself the space, support, resources, relationships and time to manage those insecurities and doubts healthfully. I did not get this trust from another person, but from myself. That is not to say I didn't have partners and role models to observe and practice with—I did. But they did not "impart" their ability to trust upon me; I relearned it. What they did is give me opportunities to take some risks and manage those risks intelligently and more strategically.

I am happy to say I now trust myself and have developed a healthy emotionally stable relationship with myself, which puts me in a position to have that with others.

The key is; I can now go first. I figured out I was not going to have a healthy relationship with someone else until I had one with myself. So when I say "think for yourself, and talk to yourself" I am literally telling you to take the time to unplug from everyone and everything. This can be for moments of time, and does not have to be for decades. Just stop for a moment throughout the day and listen inward.

In order for this to work, for me anyway, I must get out of my head. When I do, this allows me to reconnect with my inner-self and inner knowing and regain my balance. I take time daily and in many cases multiple times daily. It just feels good to me to be with me. I am now my favorite person to be with—well, most of the time and when I am not, that is usually because I'm hungry or tired. What I suggest is to sit with yourself often, in a quiet inner space and listen to your best self. After some practice, you'll find you can still hear it even when others are shouting at you. This has taken me years to get comfortable with and let me tell you, it has been worth EVERY ounce of effort.☺
By the way, when I say 'stop and listen to your inner voice', I am not talking about spending time with your *programmed inner*

*critic.* That voice needs to be told to *zip it*!! That noise is not from your inner self and is not you. That is programming and/or beliefs that have been drummed into your head by some well-meaning person or people. They really did mean well, but those harsh critical voices are not the voice of your wise inner self!

The inner self voice is ALWAYS gentle, kind and clear, and it ALWAYS feels good when you hear it, ALWAYS!!! If you are hearing a voice in your head and it feels bad to listen to it, my experience is, that is *old programming* rearing its ugly head. Go ahead and tell that voice to *zip it*!!!! It's rather liberating to finally tell that person whose been criticizing you for all these years *(in your head)* what you've always wanted to say to them, *zip it* or shut your; trap, pie hole, big mouth or some derivative of that. Try it in your mind and see what happens. What do you have to lose? That negative program, that's what you have to lose. ☺ Remember this is the voice in your head we're talking about, not the actual person. You've got some work to do before you have that conversation.... ;)
Trust yourself you are your best advisor.

# Chapter III
## Make Up Your Mind!

*"The first step to getting what you want out of life is
this: deciding what you want."*
*- Ben Stein*

## Making your mind work for you instead of you working for it

### Quieting the voices in your head

As I mentioned in the last chapter, talking to myself is one of, if not the most, empowering clarifying and soothing things I do for myself and my sanity. Admittedly, that was not always the case. As with most people I had those *mental critics* constantly *yapping* at me.

Imagine this;
You're watching a scene from a bird's eye view or hidden camera mounted high on the ceiling with a 180° view. The scene takes place in a very large conference room on a top floor of a corporate skyscraper. Three of the four walls are dark cherry wood paneling; the fourth is a wall of windows from ceiling to floor with a view of the city below. The carpeting is dark blue with flecks of black woven into it and on it sits a long, glossy oval-shaped mahogany table. Around the table are 29 people seated in high-back leather executive chairs; the seat at the head of the table sits empty. The mix of people includes men and

women, ranges in age from 35-70, all dressed in business attire. Conversations fly—some of which are civil, while others are getting heated. There is talking, however the conversations are not discernible.

The company CEO enters the room and takes the empty seat. The CEO reaches the seat and does not sit, but simply observes the interactions. Everyone is engrossed in conversations they do not notice the CEO has entered the room. Suddenly the CEO says in a commanding voice, "Shut Up, all of YOU!" And they do! The CEO continues in a calm, respectful yet direct tone, "You are my advisors and for that I am most appreciative. However, from now on each of you is to speak one at a time and only when I ask for your advice. You are not to talk unless I call on you. Have I made myself clear?" The entire group looks at the CEO and replies "Yes."

That CEO is me and the people at the table were the chattering voices in my head. This was one of the most powerful experiences and exercises I have ever done to quiet the voices in my mind. I could feel the surge of energy flow through me as the voices were silenced and I was able to think more clearly, without all the distraction. My busy brain was soothed and my mind relieved.

## Multi-Tasking….. NOT

I've always had what I call a *busy brain*. It is very active, imaginative, a bit obsessive/compulsive at times, curious, full of wonder, hungry to know more, fast moving, doesn't miss much, a bit of a steel trap, has a strong ability to intensely focus, likes to put puzzles together, and thrives on 10-15 minute daily afternoon naps.

Over the years I discovered these attributes can work for me or against me, depending on my level of awareness and control over where my attention is given.

I used to consider myself an efficiency expert, always finding ways to get things done faster through *multi-tasking*. However, through my neuroscience studies, I discovered I never was multi-tasking and it doesn't exist. It *seems* to work in *some* instances. For instance, with trained motor skills like walking and chewing gum. However, I found out it does not work with cognitive thinking. A number of you are probably thinking... what the heck are you talking about...no multi-tasking? That seems to be the case according to the most recent neuroscience, and of course my own personal experience... no multi-tasking. At least not in the way most people use the term. Most people really think they are doing multiple things at once when in reality they are only thinking about one thing at a time, hence only really "doing" one thing at a time.

Scientific studies suggest that the brain is capable of doing one to two cognitive things at once, and even that summation is sketchy. However, what the brain is VERY good at doing is what is called *switching*. It switches from one cognitive function to another so fast it *appears* as though we are multi-tasking. If you think this is a load of hooey, try focusing on two conversations at a time, and engaging fully in both of them simultaneously. You may pick up things being said between the two and be able to piece a conversation together, but you do not get the full context or depth of both conversations. Some very important details will be missed when the brain is distracted. As Dr. Amy Arnsten has discovered in her neuroscience research as presented in the book *Our Brains at Work* by David Rock, our brains are amazing but they do have limitations. ☺

Here is an example of being dangerously distracted. Picture this:

You're driving down the highway and notice an accident being taken care of on the *opposite side* of the highway barriers. What are many of the drivers doing on *your side* of the highway?

- Slowing down
- Rubber necking
- Quick and unexpected lane changing (with no indicator lights)

How does this affect the traffic flow on your side of the highway? It usually results in a traffic jam, fender benders or at least a number of "near misses."

What do you think is the root cause of the traffic jam on your side of the highway? NO, it is not the accident. It is all the people who have allowed the accident to be a distraction from their main focus, driving on their side of the road.

I understand people are curious and studies suggest that the brain is always searching for new data. Some people want to see if they know anyone in the accident. But seriously, what are the odds? In my estimation the odds are less than a fraction of 1%. Even if they *think* they recognize a vehicle involved, what can they possibly do to help from the other side of the highway *while driving*? Emergency response vehicles and personnel are on the scene. Is there anything else they can do to help, other than what is already being done? NO. Even if they are a paramedic, or a cop or fireman, they're probably off duty AND they're going in the OPPOSITE direction.

Is this ANY of their business? NO. Does worrying change anything? NO. Does it help them? NO. Does it help the people in the accident? NO. Does it make for better drivers? NO! The truly intelligent thing to do in this situation is to MYOB. Pay attention to driving so as not to cause or be involved in an accident.

## Managing Distractions - Get that dog on a leash!

Okay, so a little more about the brain. The brain is wired for new learning, it loves it and it feeds on it. It is an input seeking machine. This has its advantages and disadvantages. I have noticed this works for me in situations where everything around me preserves my safety, well-being, and in some instances my life. It has also brought me joy for having seen or heard something beautiful or amusing in my surroundings. It can, however, also work against me when I need to focus on something and my mind wanders off. Sometimes it may drift into the past ruminating over something, or it starts to focus on something other than the task at hand. Anyone else with OCD (obsessive compulsive disorder) tendencies will understand what I am talking about. This is where my principle of "Get that dog on a leash" comes in handy and has been priceless for me in managing my mild OCD easily and effectively.

Imagine your brain is like a dog, one that loves to explore, chase things that move, visit with other dogs, is very trainable and wants to please you. What are some of the things that tend to happen to dogs that are very curious and excitable but are not well trained? Are we comfortable letting them out of the house without a fence or on a leash? My experience is, NO. Why not? What is likely to happen if the dog runs out the front door without a fence or leash? The owner is afraid the dog is going to get hurt. We fear it won't pay attention, to its surroundings, or be distracted, and therefore less likely to see or hear a nearby danger, like a moving vehicle. At a very basic and simplified level, the brain responds to stimulus in a similar way. The longer I do not pay attention to what I am doing, the more likely I am to experience or encounter dangerous or harmful situations.

It has been my experience that the brain is very trainable. There is a term in neuroscience called *neuro-plasticity*. What this basically means is the brain is capable of continual learning and changing the neural network connections in the brain. The previous theories of the brain being fully developed at an early age and then stops learning are de-bunked. Recent Neuroscience studies show the brain has the capacity to continue to adapt and learn new things throughout life. Now, whether or not the owner of the brain is resistant or willing to learn new things is a completely different story.

We have the biological equipment to do it, the matter then becomes one of *choosing* to do it AND being more deliberate about it. When I mention scientific studies, I am speaking of the academic/scientific articles and reports I have read for my college classes, for personal enrichment, and in which I have participated, as well as my personal experiences. There are references and suggested reading in the back of this book.

So, your level of success with these principles and theories will be your own. I have found that what I get out of anything directly correlates with what I put into it. Since I was tired of working hard, I decided to start working smart.

Training my brain takes effort, time, energy, focus and resources. The payoffs and benefits for me far out measure the effort, resources and output I've invested.

I can now allow my dog (aka my brain) to walk the neighborhood without a leash and for the most part it stays close. When it does get distracted by something and takes off, it doesn't take much more than a whistle or a call to bring it back. There are those odd occasions when it is a little tougher to get my mind back to center. Sometimes that is an overload of hormones (yes some chemicals can make it more difficult to reign in your brain at times) other times it's a very strong belief that is being challenged. So keep that in mind, but it is not an excuse for bad behavior. Get that dog on a leash even if you have to call a friend or the dog catcher (a professional therapist or coach) to help you!

Once you get your dog back (regain your center) make sure you give it plenty of play time, rest, good food, lots of clean water to drink and opportunities to stretch and explore new things. Make this part of your regular routine. Do these things and your brain will serve you well, for life. ☺

## Using Your Imagination On Purpose! - Yes, I'm asking you to "Make Believe"

There is a phrase I hear often these days; "You get what you think about." In my experience, I have found that to be an accurate statement, however not complete in and of itself. This is not a one-time hit type or scenario; it is a progression and evolution of thought. Allow me to explain.

Thought progresses and gains momentum and energy through sustained vibrational activation. Now I imagine you may be thinking, 'What in the world does vibrational activation mean?' Let's see if I can break it down for you.

Thinking forms thoughts. A sustained thought leads to creating an image or picture in the mind. Once a picture is formed in the mind it is likely that an emotion or feeling will be evoked. When that emotional response is sustained, it is likely to create a belief around that thought and feeling. Once a belief is formed and sustained it gains momentum and an expectation is then born. When an expectation is sustained and nurtured, a sense of knowing arises. A sustained knowing creates the space for manifestation and then the desired outcome. A relationship, circumstance, or item then shows up in your reality.

So, a singular thought in and of its self is not all that powerful. It has little substance or form. However, when we continue to think that thought, it gains more energy, substance, form and momentum. When we think on it even longer, OR with repeated frequency, it gains more momentum and begins to form an image in our minds. The imagination is now engaged. Once the imagination is engaged, and to the extent it is engaged, it affects the level of belief. Once a belief is created and sustained, the likelihood of the thought manifesting into something tangible dramatically increases.

There are numerous studies out there researching the idea of "mind over matter." One comes from well-known author and speaker Dr. Dennis Waitley, Ph. D. He is the former Chairman of Psychology, Sports Medicine Council, U.S. Olympic Committee. Dr. Waitley took the visualization process from the NASA Apollo program and instituted it during the 1980's and

1990's into the Olympic program. The process is called Visual Motor Rehearsal. They used bio-feedback and brain waves sensors to record the body's responses. The sensors were attached to the athletes while they performed their respective sport. The same athletes were then hooked up again to these sensors and asked to sit quietly, close their eyes, and just imagine practicing their event in their minds. The biological responses were exactly the same. The results showed that the athletes had the same biological responses in both the real and the imagined scenarios. Their bodies reached the same levels of performance, heart rate, breathing etc., whether they were actually running the race or just imagining it.

I'm not suggesting anyone go out and attempt to run a marathon. What I am suggesting is you play with using your imagination more deliberately. Take a few minutes several times daily and use your imagination deliberately. Imagine you're going to have a good day, an easy drive to work, a good interaction with someone, a good idea coming, a good cup of coffee or tea, a great parking space, or hearing your favorite song on the radio. Once you do that, then let yourself be open to seeing, hearing about or receiving these things. Pay attention to what I call the *bread crumbs*. Bread crumbs are your evidence that these things are coming.

By the way, in case you have not figured this out yet, everything I mentioned about using your imagination to create things wanted, can also work in the opposite way; creating things unwanted. Here is what I mean.

Should you not be more deliberate in your thinking, imagining and looking for things that feel good around you, you are likely going to notice a habit of looking for what's wrong with everything around you. When this is the case, the very same dynamic is at work. Prolonged thinking forms thoughts, which then sparks the imagination, creating pictures in your mind of the worst case scenario, which then ignites "worry" (also known as a belief), which then generates more momentum in manifesting the unwanted. The imagination is a powerful resource. Use it deliberately and it is a major asset, be indiscriminate with it and it can become a major liability.

I have discovered the imagination can create a heaven or a hell in my head, which then translates to my life. It all depends on what I am looking for in any given moment and what I choose to focus upon. It's a choice. Did I say it was easy to focus on what's working for me, especially when there seems to be so many things going wrong? NO. What I can tell you is; it does get easier with practice. I used to be one of the biggest pessimists on the planet, no joke. Always finding what's wrong with everything, especially me. That was a miserable place to live. I now understand I had a major hand (mind) in creating that less than pleasant world in which I lived. When I was able to wrap my mind around this concept and started practicing it deliberately, my life gradually got better. As I continue to practice this, my life continues to get better and better and it gets easier and easier for me to see what's right with me and the world rather than what's wrong.

This practice continues to perpetuate a wonderful world to live in. Even when things go wrong I can choose to focus on what worked and move forward. Of course I can also choose the alternative which is spending the majority of my time and energy focused on what went wrong and live in that dark world. I've come to believe heaven or hell is in the now, and it's in the mind. We have the capacity to choose heaven and we get it when we make the effort to look for what's working and follow the bread crumbs.

What have you got to lose by playing with this practice of using your imagination on purpose? A little worry? What have you got to gain? A window on life where you see and experience more of what is right in the world (and you), more feeling good, and being happy more of the time. I'd call that a worthwhile risk and a good return on an investment. ;)

## Thinking, Feeling then Acting!

Okay, I used to think emotions were something to avoid, hide and ignore. I've come to recognize this caused all kinds of trouble for me as both a child and an adult. It goes back to the socialization again. I was taught to be polite and that included not challenging adults or people in authority, even when I felt someone was creepy. My gut feelings told me to do one thing; stay away from this person! My socialized training told me to "be polite" which meant put up with this person no matter what he did. By falling into the *Be Polite Syndrome* (BPS) I ended up in some compromising and abusive situations and relationships.

In understanding the law of attraction and studying the neuroscience of leadership, I have come to a new understanding of the role of emotions in my life. I now know emotions are part of my internal navigation system, or *Global Positioning System* (GPS). For some of you this is no surprise at all, you've always known that your emotions are telling you something about your perception of the world around you. For many others, including me, that was not the case. I was lead to believe that emotions were a nuisance at best and a dangerous curse at worst. Neither scenario seemed advantageous to me so I did what I could to ignore them, stuff them and not feel them. This is what I call *Emotional Trash Compacting (ETC)*. Little did I know what an exercise in futility that was. For decades I was a human *Emotional Trash Compactor*.

It wasn't until 2008, yes very recently, that I was introduced to the concept of emotions being part of my inner GPS. Through my studies and practicing these new techniques for harnessing the power of my emotions, I started to embrace my emotional responses. I've come to realize it is not only healthy to feel and identify my emotions and understand how they work, but that it is essential to my well-being. I have a whole new outlook on life and navigating it has become easier AND more fun! I am a much happier person for doing so.

Here are a few tips and tricks that helped me better understand how this works and how to apply it. Remember, I don't have all your answers. If none of these things work for you, go find your own way of doing it. You know what's best for you.

Emotions give us signals all the time in response to what's going on around us. My experience has been contrary to the popular belief that my emotional responses are generated by what's going on outside of me. I've come to recognize that my emotional responses are triggered by what's going on in my own head, by my own thoughts and thinking.

My thoughts, beliefs and expectations trigger my emotional responses. Yes, any situation or circumstance may be a catalyst. However, it is always my thinking that triggers the emotional response. When my thinking is in alignment with my true intentions or desires, it feels good; I experience positive emotions. When my thinking, beliefs or expectations are not aligned with my true intentions or desires it feels bad, I experience negative emotions. Simply put, when I think poorly I feel poorly, when I think well I feel well.

For some of you this is nothing new. You've known this forever and have generally been living happily ever after. However, some others may be struggling with this idea, like I did at first. I liken that to socialization and other outside influences (family, teachers, religion etc…) that convinced me that suffering was the purpose of life. Which I now know is not true. To those of you who have always known life is supposed to be fun, well done, keep going. To those of you for which this is new, my question to you is, "Would it be okay with you to feel good (or at least better) more often?"

If your answer is 'No, I am not ready to feel good (or at least better) more often', you have every right to that and there is nothing wrong with you. It's just where you are now. When you're ready you'll make your move. ;) For those of you who said 'Yes, I do want to feel good (or at least better) more often', I've got something you may want to try.

To help bring this concept into a physical context I've got an exercise for you. This exercise is intended to help you experience the connection between your thinking and your emotions on a visceral level.

This is **a two part exercise. Read the instructions first then try the exercise.**

Here are the instructions:

**Part 1:**

1. Take a moment to **think about something you DON'T like**; sitting in traffic, annoying people, smelly feet, eating broccoli… whatever comes to mind. Those of you with OCD, just pick one. ☺ BTW I'm not picking on you, I live with OCD too so I understand how difficult it can be to choose one thing sometimes.

2. **Think about this thing long enough to evoke a feeling within yourself.** Depending on how much you dislike this thing will determine how long you have to think about it before you feel something.

3. **Once you feel something, ask yourself "Does it feel good or bad when I think about this thing?"** If you are struggling with identifying whether it feels good or bad, here are some tips;

   i. If it doesn't feel pleasurable, it's not good.

   ii. Mild unpleasantness or discomfort is sufficient. There is no need to feel awful or depressed to get the point of the exercise. ☺

Okay, now let go of that thought/thinking, we're done with it. Some of you may have really gotten into this part of the exercise, which left your dog off its leash. You'll want to get your dog back on its leash before moving on to part 2. Once you've done that, move on.

**Part 2:**

1. Take a moment to **think about something you LIKE**; a favorite fragrance, friendly people, loving animals, a good glass of wine, walking on the beach, your best day EVER….. ;) again those of you with OCD, just pick one ☺

2. **Think about this thing long enough to evoke a feeling within yourself.** Depending on how much you like this thing will determine how long you have to think about it before you feel something.

3. **Once you feel something ask yourself, "Does it feel good or bad when I think about this thing?"**
   i. If it is soothing it's good.
   ii. Feeling pleasantness, comfort or relief are GREAT.

If you did the exercise and were able to experience the connection between your thinking and emotion, you now have yet another tool in your tool box and you know how to use it.

If you did not get the experience and would like to, keep playing with this. If you are like me, a current or former ETC (emotional trash compactor), it will likely take a bit more practice for you to get there. Since us ETC's tend to cut off our awareness of our emotions; it takes a bit longer to strengthen those connections. I promise if you practice you'll get there—just keep playing with it.

For those of you who did not do the exercise and could not care less, ignore everything I just said and go about your business… every exercise and every tool is not for every-body… ;)

Okay… so we've covered the first two pieces of this puzzle, think and feel, so where does the act come in? For some of you this may be obvious and for others maybe not. I was one of those for whom this was NOT obvious, so for those who fall into the second group, you're not alone.

When thoughts and feelings are in alignment, meaning it feels good, then what action to take becomes the next logical step. When they are NOT in alignment the opposite effect occurs. This goes for small daily activities as well as larger decisions. Let me share a few examples with you. Let's start small first.

In Chapter 2 under the heading "Listen to Your Inner Voice" I explained how I started programming parking spaces at work every day while living in Los Angeles. Little did I know at the time I was applying this principle. I would think about finding a close free parking space, just before leaving the house. I would perpetuate that thought long enough to experience how good it felt to find such a spot and then I would sense how to proceed on my commute. Sometimes I noticed I hit every light red (or green) and practiced trusting that this was all part of the plan. When I got closer to the neighborhood I thought about which street to take, and followed the best feeling path which would lead me to a suitable parking space.

That may seem very trivial or trite to some of you and you are welcome to your opinions. I never said this was going to be an action packed thriller. The reason this is important is these baby steps helped me to build my confidence in applying this theory to larger endeavors. Here is an example of a more complex situation that includes taking what I considered to be a bad decision and making it work for me.

I bought a house at the top of the real estate bubble. I never wanted a house for myself; I prefer to be much more agile. But I thought it would be a good investment and provide security for my God children should something happen to their mom (my sister) before they turn 18. I had noble intentions. Admittedly I had my reservations about buying the house and lots of clues that I ignored along the way. The house was out of state so I flew out to see it after putting it under contract. When I pulled into the driveway I looked up and thought "What the hell am I buying?" It wasn't a dilapidated shack, but it was certainly not what I expected. Going against my better judgment and feeling the pressure of BPS, I went through with the purchase. The buyers' remorse started settling in after about 2 years of ownership. Five years later I was still irritated and it was at that time I was introduced to the concept of "Think, Feel then Act" and decided to give it a try.

I was tired of living with regret and being frustrated about owning the house. I decided I wanted to change my thinking from 'buying the house was one of the dumbest things I'd ever done' to thinking 'buying this house was one of the smartest things I've ever done'. By shifting my focus away from what I didn't want and towards what I did want, and maintaining that focus, new ideas started flowing in. The ideas did not come in immediately, however it was within two days that ideas began to flow. Here is where the Think, Feel then Act process came in.

As ideas started to flow, it was important for me to pay attention to how I was feeling as I pondered these ideas. Remember the intention is to find alignment with the BEST idea for me. If I cannot feel good with the idea, I am not taking any action! One of the first things that stood out for me was 'I want the house to start paying me, and not just in equity'. To identify the sweet spot I asked myself, "How would it feel to generate cash flow with the house?" legally of course. For me, I know I'm in alignment with the best idea when I think about it long enough and I get "goose bumps" or feel a surge of energy move through me. It feels REALLY GOOD!! After thinking on it for about a minute I got the goose bumps. It felt REALLY GOOD.

I continued to think about this idea of the house paying me and began to gain more momentum, feeling even better about it. Then more specific good ideas started flooding in; I could rent the house out and be a local landlord living in an apartment, or on a live-aboard boat (which was my original intention when buying the house) and save money. I could hire a property management company to rent the house out, or another option was to stay in the house and rent rooms out as in a "boarding house" or have roommates. As these ideas came I wrote them down. Then daily I thought on these ideas long enough to identify which one felt the best, eliminating those that I did not feel were in alignment.

By the way, there was research involved as well. Because I wanted to make sure I was making grounded decisions, not just acting on my assumptions, I researched what the rental market was for my neighborhood. I also calculated a rental price for my house in order to cover expenses and make a profit. I also spoke with friends in the area for some insights. These people had either been currently renting their homes out or were renting rooms out in their homes. I got well informed and came to know the difference between feelings that were grounded in alignment and reactive feelings due to misaligned thinking.

After all the clarification I decided to go with the roommate option. Through all of the research and clarification I was able to align my thinking with what I wanted and find the best path to get there. I set up a search plan, had a preliminary questionnaire for potential roommates, and enjoyed the ride in finding a suitable one. On a number of occasions, it took some effort to reign in my thinking. To do so I would remind myself to maintain my alignment and to refrain from taking action as a knee jerk reaction.

In the end it was all well worth the effort. I got a very reliable roommate with whom I am still friends. Although we are no longer roommates, while we were I helped him through the process of buying his own house in the area. He has assisted me in creating yet another legal and ethical revenue stream with the house, and this time without having roommates. This entire process has reaped more benefits for me than I could have imagined before embarking on it.

These are just a few examples of the think, feel (good) then act principle in action.

**Allow intention to be your anchor**

In describing the think, feel good, then act principle there is one other thing that is essential to this principle's effectiveness; and that is intention. Intention can be a powerful grounding agent for our thoughts, feelings and actions. When we think, feel good and then act from a place of clear positive intention (to be happy or feel better), life tends to get easier. When we lose sight of our intention things can get very cloudy or down right muddy, and decisions can become difficult and even miserable.

Generally speaking when I lose sight of my intention, it is a sign that I am out of alignment. I have been distracted and have temporarily pinched myself off from my true self. In those moments, days or years, I am living from a programmed place rather than a place of authenticity. Each time I remember my intention – which is to feel good and be happy – I am able to reconnect with my true essence. At that moment decisions become clearer and life a little easier and better. In those moments of alignment, access is granted to a universal energy that is larger than life, providing support, resources and insights to getting to what I want easier, faster and with more fun.

For the majority of my life it has been my intention to connect with the world around me in fun, positive and meaningful ways. My world includes myself, nature, the beauty of this planet, animals, other people, financial abundance, physical and mental wellness, and ideas that stretch my imagination creating a sense of adventure, to name a few. Here is a story of how this intention manifested in my life recently.

It was a Saturday afternoon and I was at home. I had plans to do something with my boyfriend at the time and was watching a show called *Globe Trekker* on PBS while waiting for him to arrive. The destination for this episode was Puerto Rico. I was amazed at how beautiful it was and how easy it was to travel there from the U.S. east coast. My boyfriend arrived half way through the show and we watched it together. He was in the U.S. Navy at the time and mentioned that he's been there a few times. He didn't have anything nice to say about his visits to Puerto Rico, but did find some of the activities the host participated in rather intriguing. I was enchanted, energized and inspired to go there. Several times throughout the show I told my boyfriend, "I'm going there." At the end of the show I said, "That's it! I am going!"

Although he acted supportive I could tell he was not convinced. I had not taken a real vacation in over five years and I was well over due. I was so inspired and alight with the idea of going to Puerto Rico for a vacation I could feel the energy moving through me. I was getting aligned with this trip. This was in early February 2013.

I had no idea how I was going to make this happen while balancing the rest of my financial goals, but I've come to know that is not my work. That is the job of the *Law Of Attraction* (LOA). I was excited about the possibilities and remained focused on my intention which was to feel good about the trip, allow myself to have fun and go on an adventure. So I started doing my research, looking up some of the things mentioned in the show by looking up activities that were interesting to me and unique to Puerto Rico. I found a number of things which continued to build the good feeling energy around going on this trip. I was moving from hopeful to believing. As I investigated flights, lodging, rental cars, activities, and practiced my Spanish, I imagined myself being there and the good feeling grew.

One of my friends at work is Puerto Rican and grew up there and I mentioned going there to her. She became very animated and excited for me and gave me some great ideas. She sparked my interest even more, giving me ideas on obtaining inexpensive flights, reasonable rental cars, places to visit, food to eat, and things to do. The next thing I did was check my frequent flyer miles. I had enough miles to get a round trip ticket to San Juan and back, so that was checked off the list.

The next thing I investigated was the things I wanted to see and places I wanted to visit. Vieques Island was on the list. It had been featured on the *Globe Trekker* and it was a must see for me. As I investigated the island by surfing the web, an advertisement banner to the right popped up for a rental home on the island. My inner voice told me to look at it. Now, this was VERY out of character for me. I usually stay in youth hostels or guest houses when I travel abroad to conserve funds for other things. My lodgings are generally rather modest, however this time I was *inspired* to look at this house and I did. It was beautiful and in my estimation, priced VERY reasonably for what I was getting. The only problem was it was only available for 4 of the 7 days I planned to be in Puerto Rico with a 4 day minimum. I bookmarked it in my favorites anyway. I looked at the house many times, read about the owners who lived in Washington D.C. (practically my neighbors) and got a REALLY GOOD feeling about them and the house.

I decided to take the plunge and booked the house on Vieques for the 4 days. It felt so good I knew I was headed in the right direction. I decided to leave the lodging on the main island open; since it would only be for 3 days I'd wing it. Now THAT is not out of character for me. It is typical for me to travel, including abroad, without lodging reservations. So I continued making my plans, put in for the vacation time at work and got it approved, booked my flights and the rental cars for both the mainland and Vieques, and paid for the house rental. I was going to Puerto Rico and it felt GREAT!!!!!! All the pieces "fell" into place with minimal effort. Here is where it gets really good.

I was planning to pay for the trip out of my savings, which was modest already, when something incredible happened. One week before I left I was notified that I would be receiving a bonus at work.

I had no idea I was even eligible, annual bonuses were not mentioned when I was hired. The funny thing was the amount of the bonus was the amount of money I planned to spend on the trip, almost to the penny! I didn't have to dip into my savings and I would not have any credit card debt after the trip. It was paid for in cash. This is not the first time I've had something like that happen, but this was one of the biggest unexpected pay outs I've received to date. That is the LOA in action.

In the middle of all this my boyfriend and I had decide to end our dating relationship and remain friends. In late March we made plans to catch a movie together. While catching up prior to leaving for the theater he asked me if anything new was going on. I said, "Yeah, I'm going on vacation in 2 weeks." He was curious and said, "Nice. Where are you going?" I said "Puerto Rico." At that point his curiosity turned to surprise. I said a little sarcastically, "You didn't believe me when I said I was going."

He said, "I did, I just didn't think it would be so soon." I replied with a twinkle in my eye and a knowing grin saying, "You don't know me very well."

So I went to Puerto Rico by myself knowing no one there, and had the time of my life. I met wonderful, generous people every day, visited fabulous places, had a few unexpected adventures that were very exhilarating, including driving up a winding narrow mountain road flanked by 30 foot tall bamboo, driving at above normal speeds to keep up with another car to avoid getting lost!   I even got hooked on Puerto Rican coffee and I am generally not a coffee drinker!  One of the best trips of my life… and I am looking forward to how the next adventure will unfold.

Allowing your intention to be your anchor is a simple principle, however it is not a simple answer—it takes effort at first. The intention is to feel good and that means focusing on feeling good, then directing your thinking and actions *in the moment* to generate and maintain that good feeling.  I promise the effort exerted to maintain this space of feeling good pays back 1000 fold, and the more you practice the easier it gets. The more I do this the more I notice my life just gets better and better and better.  Give it a try; you've got nothing to lose (except maybe feeling crappy) and everything to gain in feeling good.

# Chapter IV
## Mind Yourself; Unplug from Reality

*"Seek understanding where reality meets the myth"*
*- Unknown Author*

### Take time to recharge your batteries

I can always tell when I am in need of "recharging" my batteries because I get cranky over little things. For me recharging my batteries has to do with maintaining a healthy relationship with myself. Making sure my needs are met, be they physical, mental, sexual, sensual (and yes those two are different) emotional or spiritual. Having a healthy relationship with myself means taking time out for me.

Just the other day, I planned to go to yoga class and ended up getting a phone call as I was leaving the office. I took the call because it was from a client 3000 miles (and 3 time zones) away and we've had a hard time coordinating our schedules. We talked for 15 minutes which then pushed my window of making it to class on time to the limit. Traffic then killed it. I really needed some exercise and it was a rather warm day (92°) so, I decided to take a walk on one of my favorite beaches. As I was driving to the new destination, I imagined putting my feet in the cool water. The feeling was so delicious I knew it was the right choice. I spent about 40 minutes there. Walking in the water and on the sand was good exercise for my body. Being outdoors on such a beautiful day was calming to my mind and helped me get into a place of appreciation. I also met a friendly woman with whom I chatted for some time. Just having that short conversation reminded me that the world is full of good people everywhere I go. It was refreshing, re-energizing and relaxing all at the same time. The only regret I had was that I did not have my bathing suit with me. I vowed to keep one in my gym bag along with a clean towel. ☺

Other ways I recharge my batteries is by listening to uplifting lectures, seminars or audio books, as well as reading the same types of materials. Sometimes it's a good novel. This gives my mind a chance to get out of what's going on in the world around me, especially when I've been focusing on what is displeasing. This creates a healthy mental distraction from what I don't want, making it easier to see what is pleasing again. This is how I am able to maintain my positive outlook and good feeling place, by unplugging from the drama in the world over which I have no control. That usually means spending time by myself, with myself, taking care of myself. In other words—minding my own business.

The other thing I do for myself is meditate. Meditation comes in *many* forms. As I've mentioned before I have a very busy brain and trying to sit for any amount of time without thinking is damned near impossible for me. Knowing this, I explored other means of meditation. The first one I discovered, which worked really well for me, was T'ai Chi Chih. I was teaching wellness classes at a local community college in Colorado and noticed a T'ai Chi Chih class on the roster. The description was a moving mediation described as "Joy Through Movement." Since seated meditation had never worked for me, I decided to give this a try. During the practice I noticed that when my body was in deliberate motion—meaning my mind was focused on my body and what was going on in it during the practice—my mind would slow down, get quiet and be more aware. It is hard to describe, but by focusing on one thing my mind was able to be aware of much more going on around me without focusing on any of it. This for me was the physical feeling and experience of meditation. In those moments I was conscious of the connection between my body and my mind. With some practice I was able to recognize this sensation easily and was later able to recreate the same experience through seated meditation.

The effectiveness of *unplugging* has also been noted in professional studies. One of these studies involved extended outdoor leadership training courses. Groups of high level executives participated in a number of river rafting, camping, or other types of multiple day overnight outdoor excursions. On these trips the participants were not allowed to bring any electronic devices with them; no computers, no cell phones, no gaming equipment, nothing that would allow them access to information outside of what they could glean from their immediate surroundings. Distractions were minimized and in most cases eliminated. What these high level executives experienced amazed even them.

They reported that by the 3$^{rd}$ day of being *unplugged* they noticed remarkable increases in their mental and physical energy levels, more mental acuity, improved problem-solving and increased creativity and resourcefulness. They also noticed they were able to remain in a relaxed state of mind longer, were more aware of their surroundings, less anxious and more refreshed.

# Be kind to yourself and patient with the process

Being kind to yourself is essential while learning how to think better and live from a place of authenticity. I lived with a very critical voice in my head for most of my life. When things would go wrong, the first thing I did is blame myself and assume all of the responsibility for what happened. Then the mental self – flogging would begin..... 'You did it again! What is wrong with you? You can't do anything right!' You get the picture. So, try to imagine what it was like when I tried to learn something new with that kind of "bully" in my head. To reduce those repercussions, I avoided letting others see me make mistakes whenever possible. When I did make a mistake I would come up with some clever explanation (or excuse), or blame someone or something else. If someone asked me I would not flat out lie about it, but I may have withheld information, and if they didn't ask, I didn't tell.

Finally at the suggestion of one of my mentors I went through a process of forgiving myself and letting myself off the *being perfect* hook. This helped me learn how to own my part in mistakes. I also learned how to stop taking full responsibility for everyone else's part in the mistakes. My mentor suggested I write a prayer of forgiveness to myself, about myself, and for myself. Once written I was to read it to myself out loud every day until I believed it and owned it. Well, as I mentioned I am not a highly religious person and the word "prayer" seemed a bit preachy to me, but I wanted to feel better so I tried it. I wanted this "prayer" to say what was meaningful and healing for me without feeling preachy.

I bought a book by Marianne Williamson titled *Illuminata; A Return to Prayer,* to help get me started. After all, what did I know about writing a prayer? It took me about a week to write it and it was worth all the work. I started reading it every day at the same time in the morning as part of my "getting ready for the day" routine. It felt a bit awkward at first but I stuck with it and pushed past the awkwardness. Within the first week of reading it aloud, I started to feel a shift of less anger and anxiety. That was the first payoff for the work I was doing. By the end of the 1st month I felt the joy and appreciation starting to creep into the spaces created within me, where the anger, anxiety and fear were moving out. I knew this was happening because I started to feel all of the self-imposed pressure to be perfect releasing its grip on me. That was the second payoff.

Slowly and steadily the inner critic was losing its volume and significance. I was starting to hear a much gentler and kinder voice. It felt so good to hear this voice, I chose to block out the critic more and more. This was the ultimate payoff for me, to feel love like I had never felt it before—moving through me, to me and from me. I then knew unequivocally that I was well on my way to living life from a place of love and appreciation while letting go of living life from a place of anger and fear. I continued this process for about a year and it was worth every minute; the effort exerted to reach this place of self-acceptance and love.

There are many ways in which my *inner life coach* communicates with me. How do I know it is my coach communicating with me? The communication is ALWAYS gentle, loving, kind, inspiring, soothing, appreciative, supportive, adoring or helpful, and in many cases humorous in a way only I would understand. Kindness and love now flow to me and from me far more easily, and patience is far less a necessity since appreciation is now my dominant focus. As I keep saying, life just gets better, and better and better.

## Allowing room for Change - in other words - Going with the flow.

I imagine a number of you have heard of the Serenity Prayer. If not here it is;

"God, grant me the serenity to accept the things I cannot change,
The courage to change the things I can,
And wisdom to know the difference."

This, in my mind, translates to "go with the flow." This concept eluded me for some time. I'd invoke it on occasion when it was convenient or I was 'knee deep in it', but I didn't understand the value of it for some time. This goes back to what I mentioned about trusting myself in Chapter II and again, socialization. The common belief that I was supposed to work, struggle, or suffer for everything was common in my family. Therefore struggling, working hard, and suffering became part of my make-up. Thankfully I was able to undo that training and come back to my senses. Working smarter rather than harder is my new way of life. ;) So some of you may be asking, "How did you do that? How did you undo that training?" It's simple—I talked myself out of it. Yes, you heard me right. I talked myself out of it. Here's one example of how I used this technique.

A number of years ago while I was beginning my studies in the LOA I was working at a local community college as an adjunct faculty member in the workforce development division. As I learned new things in my LOA studies I would practice putting these principles into action every time I saw an opportunity to do so. Well, my place of employment was one of those places ripe with opportunities. No one there knew what I was doing except for me so there was no outside pressure to be perfect. All they could see, if they were paying attention, was that things just seemed to keep working out for me.

While working at a college, the grant project I was working on was coming to a close as was the funding. This meant one of my sources of income was about to be reduced, dramatically. I had six months' notice. I did the typical things most folks do when faced with a looming income source reduction, I looked for other sources of income (aka; jobs) while continuing to deliver on my current project. What most people did not know is I was also doing something else very few people do in these situations; I was staying focused on my well-being rather than the potential loss of it. This was new for me. It took effort and practice and the payoff was greater than I could have ever imagined. When I thought about the project ending, I started to get nervous. I would then practice soothing myself by saying things like, "You've been in this position before and you came out alright, you'll be okay this time too." In those moments I would remember my past successes and it would reengage my confidence to handle this situation just as well. By month three in the count down the prospects of getting an extension on this project were slim. By day 30of the countdown mark, an extension was off the table. I remained calm and continued on.

My supervisor at the time told to me she wanted to keep me in the division and was looking for something for me, but there were no guarantees. I kept my options open and continued to look for suitable jobs in the pay range I needed to maintain my lifestyle. Mind you, I would get nervous when I thought of the loss of income; however, I never allowed that to be my dominant focus. When I felt myself getting nervous I immediately, and I mean IMMEDIATELY, soothed myself by recalling previous times in my life when I'd been in similar circumstances and came out of it just fine. What I was actually doing was redirecting my thinking away from the lack of something and towards the having of it until I felt relief. I was consistently making sure I kept my dog on its leash. This took effort and conscious awareness. I found myself regularly catching my mind wandering down the anxiety path and would stop what I was doing, catch it, and bring myself back to the present. I must have done this 50-100 times the 1st day, then as I got better at this technique, I found my mind more able to stay in the moment more often, and I didn't have to exert so much effort to keep my dog on its leash. My dog was getting very well trained to stay close.

Well, it was three weeks prior to the cut and still nothing was offered. Yet somehow I knew everything would be alright and continued to remind myself to *go with the flow*. I did look at my finances and knew I had enough money in savings and retirement funds to carry me for a few months if needed and that reduced my anxiety too. Listen, I am not saying I have a magic wand and just thinking positive does it all the time. I had to pay attention to what actions were appropriate for the situation and be prepared to take them. So, there are practical pieces of the equation that are part of making this formula work. It was my responsibility to make sure I was investigating and utilizing every resource and tool at my disposal without forcing things.

Finally, two weeks prior to the project end date I was offered a position in an area of the division I'd never worked in before and knew very little about. When the department coordinator came to make me the offer she said, "I know you are accustomed to making a certain amount of money. I can only offer you this amount hourly," then she showed me the offer. When I looked at the offer it was a 20% increase from what I was currently making. It was obvious to me that this person was not aware of my current salary so I graciously and humbly said, "I can work with that amount." All the work I'd done to keep myself grounded and centered throughout this process paid off. And that's not even the end of it, this gets even better.

So I go to this department and find out that the rest of the staff uses pagers and are on call 24/7. That bothered me a bit and made me start thinking, "What the 'H' have I gotten myself into?" I got myself together and explained that there was no need for me to be on a pager or available 24/7, especially since I was part-time and getting no benefits. The supervisor didn't like it but could not argue with my logic and dropped it. Then, they couldn't even figure out what they were going to do with me and left me to "figure something out." So I occupied an office and made myself useful for the time being, however I was still thinking 'what in the 'H' am I doing here?' Let me tell you, all the effort I put into my *go with the flow* training was really being tested at this point. There were many times when I was ready to walk out of that job, when my inner coach would say, "Just take it one day at a time." I would remind myself to *go with the flow and* again *trust* it would work out. I told myself "It will not be like this forever, there is something much better brewing."

After three weeks of dealing with this ambiguity, I was called into my supervisor's office and asked to consult on an RFP (request for proposal) for a contract with a local business partner. This agency was looking for some customized training for their clients. Little did I know where this would lead, but I decided to *go with the flow* and agreed to the meeting. I knew very little about the agency or the clients but the project was in my realm of expertise. I prepared for the meeting doing my research on the agency and prepared my questions and curriculum portfolio. I met with the directors and presented them with some ideas that met their criteria. By the end of the meeting my confidence was sky rocketing. This was not only the type of project I'd been waiting for—it had the potential to be a dream job for me.

I was a bit nervous because it was a much bigger project than anything I'd done before. This agency had a different type of clientele than I'd ever worked with in a setting that I knew would be both demanding and challenging professionally and personally. It got nervous thinking about it as I was not sure how I would make it work. When they asked me to design, develop and deliver the program I accepted it without hesitation. Again, I somehow knew this was a fantastic opportunity for me to stretch myself beyond my current perceived limits.

This was once again a contract position, meaning I would be paid for time spent in the classroom. I was not sure how they would work the contract, which again made me a bit nervous. I soothed myself over that and then came the salary offer. Wouldn't you know the offer that came in was an additional 80% increase per hour? *More* than what I was currently being paid, which added up to 100% per hour pay raise in *less than thirty days*. This blew me away. Not only did I get a huge jump in pay, I got a lot of other benefits. I no longer had to do a job I could not stand, I was allowed to do work I absolutely loved to do every day, I got to be creative in my work, had loads of autonomy (which suits me well), got to work with people I truly enjoyed working with and had endless opportunities to make a positive and meaningful contribution to my community. From where I stood, it just doesn't get any better than that.

These were just some of the payoffs for going with the flow. After I signed on the dotted line, I knew I could not have done a better job of "making" that happen by trying to control or orchestrate everything myself. What an amazing experience!! That contract went on for me for over three years and I continue reaping the benefits of having worked on the program still; five years later.

This is just one example of how learning to go with the flow has paid off for me a hundred-fold. I dare you to try it.... What have you got to lose?

# Chapter V
## Happiness is a Choice

*"You are always only one choice away from changing your life."*
*- Anonymous*

## You only have two choices; To Be or Not To Be…..Happy

This is a simple concept. It is not complicated although I have seen many people, including myself, try to make this very complicated.   When I say happiness is a choice I mean that literally, it's a choice. I have come to understand that happiness is not a final emotional destination, but rather a consistent state of being. It has been my experience that happiness is more a state of mind and can be triggered by our thoughts and attention.

Now I've also come to realize that the mind is a double-edged sword. As happiness can start in the brain so can unhappiness. Through dealing with my own personal experiences and after working with hundreds of clients, and thousands of students, I've come to a place of seeing happiness as one of only two choices – to be happy or not. I realize this may seem like an over simplification, so I want to clarify this by acknowledging that there are *levels* of happiness and unhappiness. What I've discovered is when I do not have any strong emotions about something it's usually not important to me. However, all it takes is for me to think about something long enough to evoke an emotion, to find which side of the happiness or unhappiness scale I am leaning towards in the moment.

If I *feel* good, that is an indication that happiness is where I'm headed. If I *feel* uncomfortable or bad when I think about that thing, it indicates unhappiness is right around the corner. Yes, again a simplification…. but really, it is that simple. As soon as I stopped making it so complicated, I started to lean more in the direction of happiness more often. Through this practice I have come to a place in my life where happiness is my *dominant choice*.

Some of you may be wondering how I got to this place. It is simple, I changed my mind (and I do so often). When I read or hear something on the news or in conversation and find myself thinking about it, or discussing it and feeling frustration, concern or worry, that is a clue (or bread crumb). That is when I consciously stop what I'm doing for a moment. I either change the subject in my mind to relieve the tension, or start to rework my thinking right then and there. That's how I get my dog on a leash in the moment.

There are so many things going on in the world around us. Some of these things we can control and many more are out of our control. When I find myself getting all wadded up about something I have no control over, I take a step back and stop that thinking process. To do that, I might take a deep breath or two, move my eyes to a picture or positive phrase in my space, get up and move from my current physical spot, take a drink of water, pet my cat, turn off the TV, turn on some music…. anything that can act as a temporary distraction to help me get my dog back on its leash. In that moment the only thing I do have control over is me; and that includes my thinking. I've learned that getting all wadded up over something I have no control over helps no one, and hurts me. Does it still happen? You bet. The key for me is to pay attention to how I'm feeling in the moment. Not so much physically, but emotionally. What is my Emotional Barometer (EB) telling me? Here's an example of a situation I recently had where I noticed my dog was off the leash and how I got it back on:

I was complaining about the seating chart for a social event I would be attending for work. Normally I am not bothered by these things, however for some reason on this day I was irritated. This little tirade went on for about ten to fifteen minutes. I was even pulling my co-workers in to it. They were doing a good job of remaining neutral so as not to inflame my ranting. These are some smart people. ☺ In the middle of my ranting I realized what I was doing and asked myself, "Is this really what's bothering you and do you want to keep going in this direction?" I stopped for a minute to ponder that and decided I wanted to get out of that mindset before it got worse. Now, even though I've been practicing this for a while it still takes some effort to reign in my brain. So, I started to look for things to like about the seating arrangements. I started to notice that there were some unassigned seats at other tables around the room that were more appealing to me. This brought me some relief which started to turn the tide.

I kept looking at the list of names and saw that there would be enough of these unassigned seats around the room to allow me to be the social butterfly that I am without being chained to a table a mile away from the dance floor and my other friends. In about five minutes I was able to get my dog back on its leash. I was then able to let it go and move on with my day, but I had to make a conscious effort to change my mind and the direction of my thinking to that of soothing relief.

In the past, before I applied these techniques I could have been annoyed all day, taking a few other people down with me. Since I've started using these techniques as part of my routine, I am more productive, satisfied, creative, enthusiastic, outgoing, confident and most of all HAPPY. I don't know about you, but I much prefer to be on the side of happy.

The point is, at any given moment I basically had one of two choices, to be happy in the moment or not, that's it. Did I say this would be easy all the time? NO, I did not. There will be situations that will challenge your ability to maintain your happy disposition. But I promise, the more you practice this in less intense situations, the better prepared you will be to manage the more difficult and complex circumstances.

Did I say this would be a one-time deal and you'll do it once and be happy forever more? NO, this is a continual process which calls for a commitment to paying attention to how you feel and moving towards happy. Do I have a set of instructions or a checklist for you to follow to make this easier? Not really, all I can offer you are my experiences and stories of success that hopefully spark some ideas within yourself—to play with this concept and apply this principle in your own life. This is an art rather than a science.

Now don't get me wrong, there will be times when unhappy is going to be the dominant vibration, and with good reason. When something happens to us or someone we love that tends to put us in a place of focusing on the loss, it is inevitable for us to feel unhappy. That is normal. How long we stay there is entirely up to us. Each of us will handle life's bumps and bruises in our own way and in our own time. What I do in those moments to help process through it is, take the hit. I allow myself to experience the feeling of the loss, identify it, label or name the emotion and acknowledge the feeling. Then and only then can I begin to look for the things that remain in my life that bring me some relief. This takes effort, especially when the injury is fresh or deep and reopened. In order to feel better, I must choose to no longer focus on and live in a place of deprivation and loss. That means I must *choose to look for and live in* a place of renewal and abundance.

Again, this is a choice and it is one I make every moment of every day to remain happy. Now, I may visit a dark place on occasion, which happens when I am not paying attention. I get distracted by some old belief system or programing, or I am just plain lazy, but the dark place is no longer my place of residence. To get out of that neighborhood, I make the choice to put my effort into remembering and focusing on what is good in my life now. I look for things around me that I can appreciate; a beautiful sunrise, a healthy body, a good cup of tea or coffee, the smell of a flower or favorite candle, having an English muffin with real butter on it with breakfast, fresh cream for my tea, you get the picture. As my focus starts to shift, so does my energy and I feel relief. I continue the process and feel a little more relief. I continue the process until I start to feel hopeful. This makes it easier to see more things to appreciate in my surroundings, and in my life.

I start to imagine good things that are coming to me in the short term; like going to the movies over the weekend, getting to work with one of my favorite clients this week, finding new books to add to my Kindle library, going to yoga class, things I enjoy. As the momentum builds, hopefulness begins to morph into belief. I start to see myself going on the Windjammer Schooner cruise I am planning, I have no idea how it's going to unfold, but I can see and feel myself there. I see myself traveling for work and enjoying myself and the new places I get to go and the great people I'll get to meet.

Now, I will tell you this does not always happen in one session. This may happen over a couple of minutes or a number of days or weeks depending on the depth of the issue and how much work I've done in the past to "clean it up." But the point is, every little step matters and makes a difference. The benefits are cumulative and compounded, so keep going!

These are all single choices that are strung together into moments in time, and these moments in time become minutes in a day, which then become hours in a day, which then become days in a week, which become weeks in a month and months in years, and those years become decades which become the time of our lives.

Every day holds opportunities to have the time of your life. It all starts with you and your choices. I choose to be happy. How about you?

## Which is more important to you, to be right or to be happy?

I used to be one of the biggest right fighters you'll ever meet. The funny thing was most people would not have recognized that because I was good at masking it with sarcasm and humor. I distinctly remember when a question was posed to me that shined a light so bright on my assumptions and right fighting habits, that it burned a hole right through them.

It was at my very first life coaches training program back in 2000. It was a live 3-day workshop in Sacramento, CA. I got there and immersed myself in this intensive program with 20+ other people from all sorts of backgrounds. Throughout the training the group was asked a lot of deep questions about themselves and we did not have the option to not answer. I could always tell when someone was trying to avoid the inevitable, including myself. A reaction may be to make an excuse to leave the room, or recite a long list of excuses why this question did not pertain to them, or they'd just lie and everyone knew it. What I noticed though, is eventually the truth would surface. I discovered that good life coaches have many ways of getting to the truth. The most amazing thing is, they do it in a very subtle, supportive and caring way. Admittedly, I pondered each one of those scenarios at one point or another in the workshop and came to recognize these as exercises in futility. I eventually came to appreciate the authenticity and the bonding that was created in the disclosure. It was not a confessional, no one was judging, it was simply an opportunity to pensively reflect out loud.

On one occasion, the answer to a question directed toward me was so crystal clear, and so matter of fact that I nearly shouted out my answer. This was such a powerful revelation for me it literally changed my life from that day forward. We were sitting in a circle and I was seated next to a woman I called *Mrs. Excuse for Everything*. She was one of those people who verbally processed everything; something I call "coughing up crap" to get to the truth. She was actually a very good teacher for me. I noticed I had a similar habit and realized how ineffective and damaging it was for me and my credibility. As the facilitator spoke, I listened intently to the conversation and the story she was telling. At the end of the story she said, "So my question to you all is, 'Is it more important for you to look good or to tell the truth?'" I had an immediate answer and I knew it was authentic and right on. So which side of that question do you think I was on at that time? If you guessed *tell the truth*, you are dead wrong. I was totally all about *looking good*!

That was the most powerful Ah-Ha I'd ever had in my life up to that date. Let me clarify something. What they meant by *look good* did not pertain to physical appearance as much as *protecting your image*. So, the question for me was, "Which was more important; protecting my image or taking ownership?" At that time, protecting my image was more important than taking ownership. Look, I was not a compulsive liar and neither was I fraudulent, I was just more concerned with protecting my image, being accepted, *and* being right. It was difficult for me to admit I'd made a mistake. Remember, I was a perfectionist and it is nearly impossible for a perfectionist to admit when they've done anything wrong or unacceptable. Even in the face of hard evidence, a perfectionist will still argue that it was due to some other factor; perfectionists cannot possibly be guilty of any wrong doing. Perfectionists are not liars in the sense of being malicious. They truly cannot comprehend how they did not think of every possible outcome and option. They are extremely hard on themselves and admittedly hard on others as well; however, it is NEVER the intention of a perfectionist to hurt others. Think of the character Sheldon Cooper from the TV show *Big Bang Theory* and you get an understanding of how this looks. ;)

At the time, because I had made a commitment to me, my classmates and facilitators to be willing to be open to what was presented, I was able to let this insight in. Previously I could have easily come up with a million reasons for why it was more important for me to look good rather than take ownership, but NONE of that even came to my mind because it was irrelevant. **This time taking ownership was so obvious AND was such a relief I chose to bask in it. It was easy to see my thinking I had to protect my image for what it was - *a habit. This habit had served me for a long time, however in that moment; I realized it would no longer serve me.***

This habit would not help me to get to where I was going, and it was time to trade it in for one that would. For the first time in my adult life I could look at something I thought was abhorrent about me and see it for what it was, just *a habit not a character flaw. This was such an incredible gift - a gift of freedom.* The amazing feeling of freedom for me was and still is nearly ineffable. This revelation was one of the most liberating discoveries of my life. I mean it when I say it changed my life forever more. In fact, I still feel the magnitude of it today, over a decade later, just as powerfully as I did the day it happened.

Okay so what does this have to do with being right or being happy? Only EVERYTHING!

In the moment of this revelation, insights began flowing to me. I now understood why I had not been reaching more success in my life when I had everything else going for me. I was not allowing myself to be, or others to see, the real me. I was afraid of disapproval at a deep level and used excuses for my bad behavior to try to gain it. This was all tied to my people-pleasing programming and my inner critic always telling me to be or do something that went against my own best judgment. I felt out of control and found myself bouncing between anger and depression as a coping mechanism. In short, I discovered I was continually trying to fit a star-shaped peg into a round hole. In that moment I not only decided I didn't want to live that way anymore, I made a promise to myself to make a shift towards living an authentic life. My reward for doing the work to change would be that incredible feeling of freedom I experienced earlier. That revelation provided the perspective that allowed me to start to change my thinking and thus my choices. My personal conviction and commitment to myself provided the platform from which I learned to better manage my right fighter habits (RFH), and most importantly, my perfectionist thinking.

So my next big thing was shifting my thinking towards feeling good, in every moment, which for me at the time meant managing my *right fighter* effectively. Remember, at the bottom of all of this was my perfectionist with some deep roots, so I took it one layer at a time. Since the right fighter was closer to the surface, I started there.

Okay, so what tools do I use to manage my right fighter?

# Step One:
## *Identify your hot buttons*

In order to manage my right fighter, aka Penelope, I had to become aware of what wakes her up, how she shows up, and when she injects herself into my thinking and conversations.

No one need be a neuroscientist or psychotherapist to figure this out. All it takes is a willingness to pay attention to your feelings in any given moment. Pay attention to what responses you have when you are feeling threatened or frightened and your responses when you feel confident and in control. The threat need not be physical, it can also be intellectually charged, in others words a *perceived* threat. For instance, I would notice myself getting triggered when I perceived someone trying to *boss* me around or tell me what to do rather than *asking* me to do something. The other big trigger for my right fighter was when I perceived myself being *talked down to,* or treated as though I was stupid. I did that to myself enough; no one else was allowed to do it. So, the first step is to pay attention to and recognize what *your* hot buttons

**Note:** It is best to **practice these things _before_ you are actually in the situation,** when *they are needed*. Call it whatever you want to; rehearsing, training or *practicing*, just do it.

Once you start to identify the hot buttons that get your right fighter engaged, practice step two.

# Step two:
## *Take a breath (or two or 10)*

Yes, take a deep breath and ask yourself "Which is more important in this moment, for me to be *right*, OR for me to *feel good?*"

Take a few more breaths so your brain can process that question in your PFC (prefrontal cortex). I have found that once I make the commitment to want to feel good in the moment, the answer to this question is always the same, *"to feel good."* This then activates my inner coach, also known as Grace, who then drives my actions and behaviors in those challenging moments towards a solution rather than the problem. Every time I am faced with one of these challenges, Grace is my safe harbor during my momentary and temporary inner storms.

Once the inner storm passes, which for me these days is usually within seconds or minutes (I am not kidding or exaggerating here) I can move into step three.

## Step Three:
### *Wait to take deliberate action.*

What I have discovered through this process is not everything needs or deserves an immediate response. Let me say that again in quotes, *"What I have discovered using this process is, not everything needs or deserves an immediate response."* This is my trick to managing my right fighter effectively. Since I have now been at this for a while, Penelope hardly ever shows up anymore and when she does, she is put into proper context.

This process made it possible to transform Penelope, my *right fighter* thinking and habits, into Grace. In fact, Grace has allowed Penelope to be freed from her self–imposed prison. Penelope's new BFF, Grace helps her to let go, relax and allow life to happen without trying to control everything. Grace takes Penelope to new places free of the guilt and shame that have plagued her for so much of her life. Grace presents herself as an intelligent, instigator of new thinking, a proponent of new perspectives and a loving and accepting presence. Grace has saved Penelope and me. Give Grace a chance. ☺

# You can have your drama or your dreams—which do you choose?

*"God grant me the senility to forget the people I never liked anyway.*
*The good fortune to run into the ones I do -*
*And the eyesight to know the difference."*
*- Gerrylea*

I have come to realize that I can either have my drama or I can have my dreams at any given time, just never at the same time. I'm either choosing to give my attention to my DRAMA – which usually translates to minding other people's business, OR I can choose, in any moment, to give my attention energy and resources to my DREAMS – aka my own business. No matter how I slice it, there are only two sides to this coin, "To be - or not to be – Happy." The continual question is "Am I minding my own business or am I minding someone else's business?" The answer to that question then helps me to set or "reset" my inner GPS. Taking care of my happiness is my business. Taking care of your happiness is your business.

So what's a secret to a happy life? – MYOB. Your happiness is your business; mind it like it matters because it does matter and so do you. ☺

# References and Recommended Reading/Viewing

1. *Colan, Lee J. Ph.D. (2012)* **Leadership Matters; daily insights to inspire extraordinary leadership.** Dallas: Cornerstone Leadership Institute.

2. *Hicks, Esther and Jerry (2004)* **Ask and it is Given; Learning to Manifest Your Desires,** Carlsbad, Hay House, Inc.

3. *Hicks, Esther and Jerry (2007)* **The Astonishing Power of Emotions; Let Your Feelings Be Your Guide,** Carlsbad, Hay House, Inc.

4. *Hicks, Esther and Jerry (2010)* **Getting into the Vortex: Law of Attraction in Action Episode XII 2010,** video recording, Carlsbad, CA: Hay House Inc.

5. *Lieberman, Matthew Ph.D., (2008)* **Getting on with Others.** Lecture presented on September 10, 2008, as part of the Neuro-Leadership Summit, Sydney, NSW, Australia.

6. *Lord of the Winds Films (2004)* **What the Bleep!? Down the Rabbit Hole.** Motion picture, LLC. Distributed by Captured Light LLC and Twentieth Century Fox Home Entertainment LLC Beverly Hills, and starring Marlee Matlin, Elaine Hendrix, Robert Bailey Jr., John Ross Bowie, Armin Shimerman and Barry Newman.

7. *Naparastek, Belleruth (1997)* **Your Sixth Sense: Unlocking the Power of Your Intuition,** New York: HarperSanFrancisco.

8. *Rock, David (2009)* **Your Brain at Work: strategies for overcoming distraction, regaining focus and working smarter all day long.** 1$^{st}$ ed. New York, HarperCollins.

9. *TS Productions LLC (2006)* **The *Secret.*** DVD www.TheSecret.tv

10. *Waitley, Dennis Ph.D,* official website http://www.waitley.com

# ABOUT THE AUTHOR

EJ is a life coach, educator, inspirational speaker and the Chief Happiness Officer of her life.

Her passion is facilitating self-empowerment. EJ's unique blend of education and training, practical experience, enthusiasm, authenticity and passion for the possible provide a dynamic, supportive and inclusive approach to facilitating self-empowerment.

*EJ can be contacted at ej.santos@live.com for more information on her coaching sessions, speaking engagements and personal development courses.*